THE HOLDIN' GROUND

The Holdin' Ground

a radio play TED RUSSELL

McCLELLAND AND STEWART

To the Uncle Bens and Aunt Lizzies who
still live in our Newfoundland outports.

McClelland and Stewart Limited
The Canadian Publishers
25 Hollinger Road, Toronto

ISBN 0-7710-7885-4

Manufactured in Canada by Webcom Limited

Foreword

My interest in Ted Russell's plays grew from an "experimental" course with a class of freshman students in English two years ago. For this course I dug up whatever I could find of worth to supplement the few available printed texts that constitute Newfoundland literature. Though we are experiencing a "little Renaissance" in painting, film making, sculpture and writing, the availability of these art works, especially the literary works, is still a problem for the teacher.

Ted Russell has written many radio plays and all of them have been produced on the C.B.C. over the years. All of his works have been performed in Toronto for the national network, and through the medium of C.B.C.'s overseas lending library, some have been performed in Australia.

It is unfortunate that these radio plays, which preserve a rich, unique, local language and portray a host of colourful and wholesome characters, are not more readily available to teachers and students. It is my experience that students not only enjoy what Ted Russell has written but that they also learn about a way of life that was a part of Newfoundland until 1949 when a change – the great hurry to emulate the life styles of others – took place. This book is published with the hope that the young student will delight in learning of the heritage of which he is part.

Clyde Rose

Preface

The Holdin' Ground was written for radio and was first produced in the c.b.c. St. John's studio for the national network in July, 1954. The late J. Frank Willis came down from Toronto to direct the production, using a local cast. Mr. Willis was a painstaking artist and spent several days here tape-recording such local noises as powder guns, sea-gull screams, a steamer's whistle and even the sound of a Bauline fisherman's 3 h.p. engine. He used these tapes very effectively to provide background accompaniment to the dialogue.

Since that date, the play has been broadcast three times. Two Toronto efforts, though technically excellent, failed to capture the Newfoundland flavour, while a more recent local production lacked the sound effects which are essential to the play's success. The original 1954 production was by far the best one, combining as it did mainland techniques with local acting.

Several attempts have been made to stage *The Holdin' Ground*, but a play written specifically for radio does not lend itself readily to stage adaptation. The writer of a stage-play has several means of communication with his viewers, including action, dialogue, pantomime, stage-settings, lighting effects, costumes and make-up; the radio-play writer must depend entirely upon dialogue, music, and sound effects. The inevitable result is that most radio plays, including this one, have too much dialogue and too little action for successful visual presentation on stage.

The writer for radio has one distinct advantage, however.

7

He can use settings which cannot possibly be imitated on stage. By a short interlude of appropriate music, he can shift his scene of activity from the Sahara to the Arctic or from the moon to Mars. This makes the radio-play even less adaptable to stage. In *The Holdin' Ground*, for example, there is a lengthy conversation aboard Ben's boat as he and Michael leave the harbour, with sound effects of water slapping against the bow of the boat, and the muted "putt-putt" of Ben's engine. In any stage adaptation, this dialogue would have to take place by Sophy's gate or on Ben's stage-head, and would be much less effective.

Despite these and other handicaps, two local Drama Clubs have succeeded in putting *The Holdin' Ground* on stage. In 1956, the Northcliffe Drama Club won the Regional Drama Festival with it, and one of the club's members won the Best Actor Award for his portrayal of Ben. A year or two later CJON televised the Northcliffe Club's performance. The Avion Players of Gander presented their stage version in the 1969 Regional Drama Festival, and in the Eastport festivals of 1970 and 1971. All these performances drew large audiences who apparently came to enjoy the play rather than to criticize its structural defects.

My comments on the play itself will, I hope, answer many of the questions which have been asked me over the years. The time of Ben's narration is July 11, 1954 – the eve of the day of the lodge meeting. His narrative deals with events which began exactly a year earlier, while Paddy Muldoon's trial took place around 1935. The places, Pigeon Inlet, Muldoon's Cove, and Hartley's Harbour, are not to be found on the map, but they contain features with which every Newfoundlander is familiar.

Was there ever a magistrate like Skipper Bob Killick? Yes. During Responsible Government days, it was customary for the authorities to appoint retired skipper-men as magistrates in our more remote areas. These men were highly respected in their communities and what they lacked in legal training was more than balanced by their sense of justice and their practical knowledge of human nature. They were all retired by the Commission of Government and replaced by younger and presumably more capable men.

For those who may be interested, the Latin tag is taken from Horace's eleventh epistle. By lifting the line out of context, I admit to having given it a meaning slightly different from the one that Horace originally intended.

Finally, let me say that any apparent criticism in the play of Newfoundland's resettlement policy is purely coincidental. The play was written more than a decade before we even dreamed of such things as "infrastructure" and "growth centres."

Ted Russell

CHARACTERS

Ben Walcott

Lizzie Walcott

Skipper Joe Irwin

Michael Shannahan

The Magistrate

Biddy Muldoon

Paddy Muldoon

The Constable

The Holdin' Ground

TED RUSSELL

BEN: (I'm sittin' on my stage-head lookin' out at where Skipper Joe Irwin's schooner is ridin' at her moorin'. And lookin' at her, I've noticed how she's always on the move. Swingin' this way and that with the tide and the baffles of off-shore wind from the hills; fallin' back till her chain brings up taut – then shootin' ahead to slacken it. Always and forever on the move. A stranger not knowin' the difference 'd think she was adrift. That is, if he didn't know about her chain and her anchor – and her holdin' ground.

And the thought struck me how much that schooner is like us people along this part of the Newfoundland coast. (And most likely, like people everywhere.) Oh, we have our little baffles of wind and tide, differences of opinion on a good many things, that swing us in different ways: A stranger might think we were gone adrift. That is, until he knew about our moorin's and our holdin' ground.

'Tis funny – the thoughts that'll run through an old fisherman's head. And another funny thing! You find a thought in your head and you wonder how it got there – what led up to it. Now, what in the world made me get to comparin' people with Skipper Joe's schooner? Oh yes. I remember. I started by thinkin' about the job I've got to do tomorrow. And that, of course, led me to thinkin' about Michael.

About Michael and me and the Holdin' Ground.)

Brief musical break.

11

BEN: (Michael. It's one year ago this very evenin' since he landed here in the mail boat from the steamer. I didn't see him that first day because I had gone in over the hill with my trout-pole. I heard the steamer blow all right, but it never dawned on me that a visitor would be on her, and besides – the trout were bitin'. The upshot was that the first I heard about it was from Lizzie. [Lizzie's my missus, though everybody calls her Grandma Walcott, just as they call me Grampa.] She was waitin' for me with the news when I got home.)

Break. Sound effects.

LIZ: (Off mike.) Is that you, Ben?

BEN: Yes, my dear.

LIZ: I wish you'd have come home a bit earlier.

BEN: I couldn't. The trout don't bite proper till almost dark.

LIZ: I get so worried with you in there by yourself. Supposin' you had an accident, or a sick turn – or something?

BEN: Nothin' no good ever comes to any harm. Look at the fine gad of trout I've got.

LIZ: My – they're lovely ones. Now, wash up and eat.

BEN: I'll take a few over to Sophy's. For her breakfast.

LIZ: Yes. They'll come in handy. She got a boarder. Come on the steamer this evenin'.

BEN: Oh. Who is he?

LIZ: I dunno. 'Twas Emma Jane Bartle that looked in and told me about him. But she hadn't found out his name.

BEN: Did she say what he looked like?

LIZ: No. Except that he was tall – with a dark suit, dark hat, dark coat – and a dark scarf round his neck.

BEN: Scarf? This time of the year?

LIZ: Yes. Emma Jane figgered he didn't look well.

BEN: But, Lizzie – didn't you see him at all?

LIZ: No.

BEN: That's a wonder, when he had to pass right along by the kitchen window on his way up the hill.

LIZ: I must've dozed off. Now, eat your supper.

Sound effects: entry and door closing.

LIZ: Oh, it's Joe Irwin. Good evenin' Skipper Joe.

JOE: Evenin' Grandma. Evenin' Grampa. Oh. Sorry. I didn't know you were havin' supper.

BEN: That's all right boy. Come. Sit in and have some.

JOE: No, Grampa. Thankee all the same. Had mine an hour ago. How was the troutin'?

BEN: Middlin', Joe. Middlin'. Got a fry and a few for Sophy besides. I'm goin' to take 'em over in a few minutes. Gives me an excuse to meet the stranger.

JOE: 'Twon't be no good. I just come from there.

BEN: Why won't it be no good?

JOE: He's gone to bed.

BEN: Gone to bed this hour? What's the matter with him? Ain't he sociable?

JOE: 'Tis not that. Aunt Sophy says he looked tired – like he wasn't a well man. I thought the same when I took his suitcase on the wharf. He could hardly straighten up with it, but when I took it – why, 'twas no heavier than a bucket of water.

BEN: He's a big fellow, though, by all reports.

JOE: Yes, tall and broad. A big frame, but not much meat on it. Like I said. A big man but not a well man.

LIZ: Perhaps he's broke down and come here for a rest. How long is he stoppin'?

JOE: Only till the steamer comes back from the norrard tomorrow evenin'.

LIZ: Only twenty-four hours. Poor boy. He won't rest up much in that time.

BEN: Now Joe, who is he and where's he from?

JOE: I dunno, Grampa.

BEN: But didn't Sophy tell you?

JOE: She don't know neither.

BEN: Well, why in the world don't she? Didn't she ask him?

JOE: No.

BEN: Well, she should have. She should have had that much pumped out of him before he was in the house five minutes. What's comin' over Soph?

JOE: Sophy says he's not the kind of man you pump. She says there's something about him. It puzzles her.

BEN: Puzzles her?

JOE: Yes. And it puzzled me too, when I brought him up here this evening.

BEN: Perhaps he's stuck-up?

JOE: No, 'tis not that.

BEN: Stand-offish?

JOE: No. Nor that neither. Like I say. It puzzles me.

BEN: Well, it won't puzzle me. I'm goin' over to Sophy's and find out the rights about him. Now.

LIZ: Now Ben, you'll do nothin' of the kind. Clunkin' around Sophy's house disturbin' the poor man when he wants his rest. Take off your boots!

JOE: Besides, Grampa you'll have plenty of chances to find out all about him tomorrow.

BEN: Why? How?

JOE: Aunt Sophy says he asked her to engage a boat for him for tomorrow.

BEN: Oh.

JOE: Yes. He wants someone to take him in boat for a few hours.

BEN: Well then, Joe – you take him.

JOE: No. He made a special point of it that he wants the oldest man he can get. That's you.

BEN: I wonder what he wants?

14

JOE: Perhaps he's a writer fellow. You know the kind who goes back and writes about "us quaint and backward people."

LIZ: No. I've never seen him, but from what I've heard already, I'd say he was more respectable than that. Anyway. Ben. You'll find out tomorrow.

JOE: Sophy's packin' a lunch basket for the two of you. She says take a kettle in case he feels like goin' ashore to boil up.

LIZ: Yes, Ben. And take care of that man. Take an oil-coat for him in case it turns wet – and the bear-skin rug. It gets airsome these evenin's. And Joe.

JOE: Yes, Grandma?

LIZ: Perhaps you'd pass these few trout in to Sophy on your way along.

BEN: And tell her I'll be ready in the mornin'. And – Joe.

JOE: Yes?

BEN: Do it quiet. Perhaps he's asleep. Restin' up for tomorrow.

JOE: I won't disturb him. Well – good night.

BEN: Oh – Joe.

JOE: Yes. Grampa?

BEN: In case I'm not back in time tomorrow, don't forget to hoist the flag for the Lodge meetin' tomorrow night.

JOE: I'll remember. I s'pose you'll be back in time for Lodge.

BEN: Bound to be. In any case, I've got to be back for the man to catch the steamer.

JOE: That's right. Well good night – again.

BEN: Good night, Joey me boy.

Break.

BEN: (Me and Grandma took it easy next mornin' and 'twas nearly eight o'clock before I lighted the fire and went down to take my boat off her collar. A lovely mornin' with just a draft of sou-westerly and one or two crews already in from haulin' their cod-traps. I got the boat ready and went back to where my kettle was boilin'. I took a cup of tea in to Lizzie. [She's poorly nowadays since the summers are chillier than they used to be.] Then I fried my trout, 'et my breakfast and sat down by the kitchen window to watch for Sophy's signal. I was on my second pipefull when she come out on her doorstep to shake out her table-cloth. So, over I went.

When I got there, he and Sophy were standin' by the gate. She told him I was her father and handed me the lunch basket. I could see that behind his back, she was twistin' her eyebrows into knots and makin' motions like tryin' to put a collar on hind part before as if she was tryin' to tell me something. But – whatever it was, I didn't twigg it – at the time. And, of course, she was too good mannered to call me aside and whisper it to me. But as it turned out, it didn't matter. Only 'twould have saved me a bit of a shock later in the day.

He was dressed just like they'd said – scarf and all, and I almost cricked my neck lookin' up at him as we walked down the path. There was that something about him, but he looked friendly enough, so I tried to break the ice.)

BEN: I take it, you'm a stranger in these parts, sir?

MICHAEL: I have never been here before.

BEN: Any of your folks livin' around here?

MICHAEL: No.

BEN: Any acquaintances, like?

MICHAEL: None.

BEN: Oh. You wouldn't be one of those writer fellows, would you?

MICHAEL: Writer fellows? Oh no,

BEN: (Well, so far I wasn't makin' much headway but on my next jig, I struck something.)

BEN: Did you have a good night's sleep, sir?

MICHAEL: I did indeed. The best for a long time. It was so quiet.

BEN: And your breakfast, sir. Did you like the trout?

MICHAEL: They were delicious. Your daughter told me you caught them.

BEN: Yes, sir – That I did.

MICHAEL: Where did you catch them?

BEN: Just in over the hill. Not ten minutes' walk.

MICHAEL: Not – ten – minutes' – walk. How I wish –.

BEN: You wish what, sir?

MICHAEL: No matter. There won't be time.

BEN: There's a long day ahead of us, sir.

MICHAEL: But there's so much to be done in just one day.

BEN: Oh.

BEN: (Well, that brought us to my stage head. Skipper Joe came around from the next stage where he and his crew were puttin' away their fish. Joe helped us get our things aboard. I reminded him about the flag on the Lodge and he reminded me not to be late for Lodge meetin' that night. Then we shoved off and his crew waved to us from around their splitin' table. After that there was no chance to do much talkin' till we were nearly out the harbour – with the engine runnin' proper and the cover down over it to cut out some of the racket. Then I said – I was at the tiller and he sittin' by me on the after thwart.)

BEN: Sir.

MICHAEL: Yes?

BEN: My name is Ben – Ben Walcott. Most folks hereabouts call me Grampa. But you call me Ben. If you like.

MICHAEL: Yes, Ben.

BEN: And now sir.

MICHAEL: Yes, Ben?

BEN: If I might make so bold, sir, what might I call you?

MICHAEL: Oh. You may call me – Michael.

BEN: That's fine. Michael. Now we're shipmates. Ben and

Michael. Well, Michael, here's the mouth of the harbour. Any special way you'd like to go? Or is one place same as another?

MICHAEL: I want you to turn north. Let me see. There's the sun. About south east. That means we're heading east right now. So turn sharply left or should I say "Hard-a-port."

BEN: Hard-a-port it is. Mike, boy. I should've knowed all along that you're a seaman.

MICHAEL: Seaman?

BEN: Yes. Ain't you?

MICHAEL: Why, no.

BEN: Never been?

MICHAEL: No. Never in my life.

BEN: A fisherman then?

MICHAEL: No.

BEN: Never in your life?

MICHAEL: Never.

BEN: Oh. Well, we're headed north straight for Hartley's Harbour.

MICHAEL: Hartley's Harbour. How far away is that, Ben?

BEN: Six mile down the shore, sir.

MICHAEL: Isn't there some place nearer than that?

BEN: No, Michael, that's the nearest. Hartley's Harbour. Six mile.

MICHAEL: But isn't there a place between Hartley's Harbour and Pigeon Inlet?

BEN: No.

MICHAEL: Ben. Are you sure?

BEN: Certain sure, sir. Why I've lived here all my life. Eighty odd year. I ought to know.

MICHAEL: Strange.

BEN: Oh. Wait a minute.

MICHAEL: Yes?

BEN: You wouldn't be thinkin' about – No. Of course you wouldn't.

MICHAEL: Thinking about what, Ben?

BEN: There used to be a place between here and Hartley's Harbour.

MICHAEL: Yes?

BEN: But 'tis not there now.

MICHAEL: What was the name of the place?

BEN: Muldoon's Cove 'twas called. But like I said 'tis not there now.

MICHAEL: Why? What happened to it?

BEN: Oh – most of 'em moved away, and those that didn't died out, till there's no one left. I remember the night they waked Uncle Paddy Muldoon. He was the last.

MICHAEL: I'd like to visit Muldoon's Cove.

BEN: But Michael, you can't. There's nobody there.

MICHAEL: Still, I'd like to go there. Do you mind?

BEN: Not a bit. Only, like I'm tellin' you, you won't see anybody there – And besides –

MICHAEL: Yes?

BEN: 'Tis a tricky place gettin' in and out of. All shoal water, muddy bottom, kelpy rocks and mussel beds.

MICHAEL: But you know your way in and out, Ben?

BEN: Of course I do. Been in and out hundreds of times.

MICHAEL: Well then, let's go in.

BEN: Another thing. There's not enough water for gettin' in and out at low tide.

MICHAEL: How's the tide now?

BEN: About half-down. If we go in there now, we'll have to bide there five or six hours till it rises again.

MICHAEL: Still – I'd like to go in – Ben.

BEN: O.K. Shipmate. Here she goes – a little bit to port.

Break. Sound effects.

BEN: Well, there's Muldoon's Cove comin' open. What there is of it. That old pine tree on the cliff is right behind it.

MICHAEL: And there's a house. Is that – the house of the man you mentioned? The last man who lived here?

BEN: Yeah. That's Paddy Muldoon's house. And his father's before him. Nigh on a hundred years old. The last one standin'.

MICHAEL: Ben! I want to do something.

BEN: What, Michael?

MICHAEL: Give me the tiller. I want to steer her in.

BEN: No, Michael. You'd run her aground.

MICHAEL: (slowly) Not if I keep Muldoon's house right in line with that tree at the top of the cliff.

BEN: How in the name of –

MICHAEL: At half-tide. I'll have four feet of water under her keel all the way in. Won't I, shipmate? Won't I?

BEN: Michael!

MICHAEL: Yes, Ben?

BEN: You said you'd never been in these parts before.

MICHAEL: That's right, Ben.

BEN: Did you mean Muldoon's Cove too?

MICHAEL: I give you my word, Ben. I've never seen Muldoon's Cove before. I'm now visiting Newfoundland for the first time.

BEN: Well, mister, whoever you are or whatever you are. Take the tiller, sir.

MICHAEL: – Michael.

BEN: Take the tiller, Michael.

MICHAEL: Thank you, shipmate. No. Don't slow her down. I'll take her in.

BEN: (And he took her in – straight as a die. With rocks almost scrapin' on both sides, he kept the roof-tree of Muldoon's house dead in line with the old pine-tree on the cliff. And the look on his face and his steady grip on the tiller told me something. Maybe he hadn't been here before – not with his body, that is, but he'd been here thousands of times – in his dreams.

And without sayin' a word, I give him the highest praise a man could give in a time like that. I kept my hands away from the engine, and made my face look as if I didn't have a care in the world.

A few minutes later, we were walkin' around lookin' at the place – what was left of it. With any other visitor I'd have been ashamed to have nothing better to show him. But not so with Michael.)

MICHAEL: You say, Ben, that the Muldoons lived here and the Cassidys lived across the Cove. Were these the only families?

BEN: Yes. Apart from the Shannahans.

MICHAEL: Oh yes! The Shannahans. And where did they live?

BEN: Just up the droke a piece. Behind where the alders have grown up. That's where their graveyard is, and where their chapel used to be. Would you like to go up?

MICHAEL: Yes, Ben. In a minute. But first tell me something about these people – these Muldoons and Cassidys and Shannahans.

BEN: (So I told him, as best I could, how, years before I was born, these three families had come to this shore from a place across the ocean that they talked about and sung about called County Galway. How they'd found the Cove and built their homes beside it. How they'd fished only because they had to, but they'd loved the soil and had cleared every inch of it from Muldoon's Cove, right up the droke on both sides of Cassidy's Brook, clear back to the foot of Shannahan's Ridge. How for two generations they'd thrived, and then – there wasn't enough land to divide among the boys, and the maidens had to leave to find life partners – How the first to go – Fergus Shannahan

– about my own age, left with his young wife Maggie O'Rourke and went to America nigh on sixty year ago. How, down the years, the Cassidys had all gone or died, and the rest of the Shannahans and all the Muldoons exceptin' Uncle Paddy and Aunt Bridget. And now they were gone too.)

MICHAEL: Ben, those that went away. Did any of you people ever meet up with any of them afterwards?

BEN: No, Michael, except once when Jonathan Briggs was in a place called Toronto twenty odd year ago and happened to run into Terry Cassidy. Terry wanted to know everything. He kept Jonathan for hours talkin' about Pigeon Inlet and Hartley's Harbour and Muldoon's Cove and givin' him all the news about Uncle Paddy and Aunt Bridget. You'll think it queer what I'm goin' to say.

MICHAEL: Say it anyway, Ben.

BEN: Well, Jonathan told me that Terry Cassidy – right there in the middle of Toronto – sounded to him like a man who was lonesome. – And homesick.

MICHAEL: That doesn't sound queer, Ben. I can easily believe it.

BEN: We've got a sayin' Michael, we fishermen here in the Newfoundland bays – a sayin' that relates to people who leave and go away to bigger cities.

MICHAEL: What is it? This saying?

BEN: It's this. We say "You can take a man out of the Bay, but you can't take the Bay out of the man." It means –

MICHAEL: I think I know exactly what it means, Ben. *Caelum non animum mutant, qui trans mare currunt.*

BEN: What kind of talk is that, Michael? That's not English.

MICHAEL: No, Ben, it isn't English. The man who first said that didn't know any English. But, when he said it, he must have been feeling very much as Terry Cassidy was feeling in Toronto. Or as I'm feeling now.

BEN: Say it again Michael.

MICHAEL: *Caelum non animum mutant, qui trans mare currunt.*

BEN: It sounds like poetry when you say it, Michael.

MICHAEL: It is poetry, Ben. And what you said was poetry too.

BEN: Me? Said poetry?

MICHAEL: Listen. Two lines of poetry.

Caelum non animum mutant, qui trans mare currunt.

You can take the man from the Bay, but not the Bay from the man.

BEN: What does the first line mean, Michael?

MICHAEL: Exactly the same as the second line, Ben. Now, let's go up back and see the cemetery, and the chapel and the place where the Shannahans lived.

BEN: (We stopped by the cemetery, while I picked up a rock and nailed on a palin' that was off the fence. Then we leaned in over while I pointed out to him whose was which among the graves.)

MICHAEL: I notice the cemetery fence is kept in good condition.

BEN: Yes. Uncle Paddy kept it up as best he could, while he lived.

MICHAEL: And since then?

BEN: Well, the truth is, Michael, I've been comin' down off and on myself to keep an eye on it.

MICHAEL: Ben.

BEN: Yes, Michael?

MICHAEL: Will you continue to – keep an eye on it?

BEN: Sure I will.

MICHAEL: Thank you, Ben.

BEN: (There was a shorter delay when we were passin' the place where their chapel used to be. There's not a trace of the chapel left, but we older fellows still remember where the built-up end of it used to be, and I pointed it out to Michael, and asked him to walk around that spot instead

23

of traipsin' over it. Then we continued on up to where the Shannahans had their place. There's nothin' left now except part of the rock wall that Fergus Shannahan's house stood on. We stood lookin' at that for a minute and once I got the foolish notion that something was glistenin' on Michael's cheek. But when I looked again 'twas gone. Besides, there was no falter in his speech, and what would a man like him find in Muldoon's Cove to affect him anyway? So back we come and sat down on the grass behind the beach with the lunch basket and tea-kettle right beside us.)

BEN: Will it soon be time to boil up – Michael?

MICHAEL: Not for a few minutes, Ben. Tell me something. You mentioned a Shannahan – the one who went away first.

BEN: Yes. Fergus Shannahan. The one that married Maggie O'Rourke from down the shore – same place my missus Lizzie come from. We met the two girls one summer we were fishin' down there. They were close friends. So were me and Ferg.

MICHAEL: You say you and Fergus fished together?

BEN: Yes, and et together and slept together. Many a time. We did everything together.

MICHAEL: Except – pray together?

BEN: Oh, we prayed together too. Indeed we did. Especially one night that I remember.

MICHAEL: Prayed together? Where, Ben?

BEN: On a pan of ice it was, Michael – about four miles off Hartley's Harbour Point. The swiles was in, and we two buckos were too far off when the wind shifted. We got cut off from the crowd and were adrift on the pan all night. Bad night too. Nor'West wind and snow.

MICHAEL: But the two of you were together.

BEN: Yes and lucky for me that we was. I slipped off the pan durin' the night, but Ferg hauled me back on. Big fellow, Ferg was – about your size. Then to keep me from freezin' he took off his own mackinaw and wrapped it round me like a blanket. Good thing for me he had two pair of socks on his feet.

MICHAEL: Why?

BEN: Why? 'Cause he took off one pair and made me put 'em on instead of my wet ones. Too big, they was, but – my feet didn't freeze.

MICHAEL: How were you rescued?

BEN: Well, all the boats come searchin' for us next mornin' but 'twas old Martin Cassidy and Paddy Muldoon that got to us first. Just in time too. Our pan had broke up a lot durin' the night, and by daylight twas no more than a clumper – likely to roll over any minute. Ferg and me learned something about prayers that mornin'.

MICHAEL: What did you learn, Ben?

BEN: Well, you know how some people think you can only pray from your heart when you're kneelin' on your knees.

MICHAEL: Yes.

BEN: Well, they're wrong. You can pray from your heart when you're lyin' flat on a slippery ice clumper, with your fingers dug into a crevice – and prayin' the clumper won't capsize while a rowboat is comin' from a mile away. Oh, me and Ferg Shannahan prayed together alright. Like we done everything else together.

MICHAEL: Didn't you ever hear of him after he left?

BEN: His wife Maggie used to write to Lizzie. But she must've died over forty years ago.

MICHAEL: Forty-six years ago last March.

BEN: Yes. Forty-six years ago last March like I said. But I'll bet neither Ferg nor Maggie while they lived ever forgot us people.

MICHAEL: No, Ben. *Caelum non animum mutant –*

BEN: Stop, Michael. Let me finish it. Say the first half again.

MICHAEL: *Caelum non animum mutant –*

BEN: *– Qui trans mare currunt.* You can take the man from the Bay –

MICHAEL: – But you can't take the Bay from the man.

BEN: Why, we've both learned something today. Now, let's see what Soph put in the lunch basket. Then I'll light a fire and we'll boil the kettle and have a mug-up.

MICHAEL: Wait, Ben. Don't boil the kettle yet. Besides, it seems a pity to disturb Sophy's lunch.

BEN: That's what it's for, Michael. Besides, we've got to eat.

MICHAEL: Ben. I'm in the mood to suggest something.

BEN: What?

MICHAEL: Mussels.

BEN: Mussels?

MICHAEL: Yes, Ben. Mussels. What about mussels?

BEN: There's plenty of 'em just out there. But what do you mean "What about 'em?"

MICHAEL: They're good to eat, aren't they?

BEN: Yes. Sure. For them that likes 'em.

MICHAEL: Don't you like them, Ben?

BEN: Who? Me? Why, yes.

MICHAEL: Did you and Ferg ever eat them – together?

BEN: Yes. Often enough. When we were boys, we'd cook on the beach and eat 'em right out of their shells.

MICHAEL: Isn't there a right time of the month for them?

BEN: Yes. Full moon – like it is now.

MICHAEL: And with the tide just beginning to rise?

BEN: Yes, by golly, Michael. Just the right time. Boiled in their shells in their own sea water dipped up on a risin' tide.

MICHAEL: Well, Ben. What are we waiting for?

BEN: We'll take 'em back home and Soph'll do 'em up in the oven with bread crumbs and cheese. You'll like 'em that way. You've eaten 'em before?

MICHAEL: No. Never. But if you and Ferg Shannahan ate 'em out of their shells, why can't you and I do the same?

BEN: Blest if I can see any reason why not. All right, wait here till I go off in boat and get a kettleful.

MICHAEL: I'm coming with you Ben. I want to pick them.

BEN: (And an hour later we had finished the last of the kettleful of mussels and I looked at him across the little pile of empty shells.)

BEN: Well, Fergie boy. They tasted good as ever, didn't they?

MICHAEL: Yes, Ben. They certainly did.

BEN: Michael!

MICHAEL: Yes, Ben?

BEN: I called you Fergie.

MICHAEL: That's all right, Ben.

BEN: But you answered. Just as if your name was Fergie.

MICHAEL: But it is my name. Michael Fergus to be exact. Call me Fergie if you wish.

BEN: No. I won't. I mustn't. Because – seein' you leanin' back there, with some colour back in your cheeks and a twinkle back in your eyes, I thought for a minute – But no. You're not over eighty years old – are you?

MICHAEL: Goodness no, Ben. I'm not sixty.

BEN: Of course not. I should've knowed better. But still, I'm not callin' you Fergie again. And now Michael, I'm off to the brook to rinse out the kettle. Then I'll be back to fill my pipe.

Break.

BEN: (After that we lay back on the grass, me with my pipe, and him with the bear-skin rug under him that I'd brought up from the boat for fear the ground might be damp to him. And because he wanted it, I told him some of the old tales of the people who'd lived in the Cove. About how Paddy Muldoon had killed the bull-moose right by his back door – of how they'd cured old Shamus

Cassidy of over-drinkin' by makin' him believe he was dead – and about Uncle Paddy's trip in the helicopter away back in the year 1892.

And Michael listened, and took it all aboard and never once did he interrupt me except to prod me when I slowed down. 'Twas in one of these bits of proddin' that he said to me.)

MICHAEL: Ben, you mentioned Uncle Paddy Muldoon's wife. Who was she before she married him?

BEN: Aunt Bridget? Why, she was a Shannahan. Ferg's sister. And she was the kindest that ever lived.

MICHAEL: Tell me more about her.

BEN: You know something about the Good Book, Michael.

MICHAEL: Yes. I ought to.

BEN: And what it says about the reward for givin' the cup of cold water in the spirit of kindness.

MICHAEL: Yes.

BEN: I suppose the same applies to cups of tea?

MICHAEL: I should think it would, Ben.

BEN: Well, then Aunt Biddy's got enough rewards comin' to her to fill the hold of Joe Irwin's schooner. Livin' in a sort of half-way house, the cups of tea she give away 'd float Joe's schooner anyway.

MICHAEL: She was hospitable?

BEN: Indeed she was. But here's a funny thing.

MICHAEL: What, Ben?

BEN: 'Twas her very hospitality that got her and Uncle Paddy into trouble with the Law – the only time to my knowledge that the law ever had to come to Muldoon's Cove.

MICHAEL: She didn't get into trouble with the Law for givin' away mugs of tea?

BEN: No. Twas mugs of black-currant juice. But perhaps you'd like to hear the full story?

MICHAEL: Yes, Ben. I would.

BEN: (So I told it, and as I did, it seemed as if my mind took me back eighteen years, and I was there again in the little court-house in Hartley's Harbour with the Magistrate, Skipper Bob Killick, on the bench. Constable Jinkins the policeman – a severe lookin' man if ever there was one. Aunt Biddy sittin' to one side, and Uncle Paddy standin' up facin' Skipper Bob.)

Sound effects: order in court

MAGISTRATE: Now Patrick Muldoon, as you know, you're charged with illegal possession of alcoholic liquor.

BIDDY: What an unchristian name to put on me drop of old berry juice.

CONSTABLE: Order in Court. Order there.

MAGISTRATE: This "drop of berry juice" as I have heard it called appears to have contained 38 per cent by volume – according to the report of the Analyst as submitted to the Court by Constable Jinkins. Do you wish to question him?

PADDY: Yes. Skipper Bob. I mean, Your Honour – This thirty what was it you said?

MAGISTRATE: Thirty-eight per cent.

PADDY: Do that mean 'twas too strong?

MAGISTRATE: Yes.

PADDY: Well then, Skip – Excuse me – Your Honour – you can blame it on the Redway's Ready Relief.

MAGISTRATE: Blame it on the what?

PADDY: The Ready Relief, Your Honour. Twas a Redway's bottle that the policeman put the little sample in to send away to the authorities, – and –

MAGISTRATE: Constable – was it a – Ready Relief bottle you used?

CONSTABLE: I didn't notice, Your Honour.

PADDY: But I did, Your Honour, and it's my opinion that our drop of berry juice is takin' the blame for the strength of the Redway's Ready Relief.

CONSTABLE: I rinsed out the bottle first, Your Honour.

PADDY: Yes – but the strength of that stuff –

MAGISTRATE: Order. In any case, Mr. Muldoon, I think it's a different kind of strength that the analyst refers to. Have you anything else to say, Mr. Muldoon?

PADDY: No, Your Honour.

BIDDY: Oh Paddy, Paddy – tell him about your heart-burn.

CONSTABLE: Order there. Order. Order in the Court.

MAGISTRATE: Mr. Muldoon – is it your wish to tell the Court about, er –

BIDDY: His heart-burn, Your Honour.

MAGISTRATE: Your heart-burn?

PADDY: No, Your Honour.

BIDDY: Well then, I'd like to tell about it.

PADDY: Now, Biddy – Biddy – darlin'.

CONSTABLE: Order there.

MAGISTRATE: Very well then, Mrs. Muldoon. Considerin' the close relationship between you and the defendant, the Court feels that you should be given every opportunity to give the – background to this case. You may sit down, Mrs. Muldoon. Now, Mrs. Muldoon, first of all, what did you mean by referring to this – er – Alcoholic Liquor as a – drop of berry juice.

BIDDY: Because that's all it is, Your Honour. You see, when the Cassidys and the Shannahans and the Muldoons – all of us – lived in the Cove – each family had his own garden, and each garden had its own rows of black currant bushes; and we shipped black currants away every year all up and down the coast by the twenty-two-pound tubful – besides havin' plenty for our own use. Then when there was only me and Paddy left we had more than we knew what to do with. You don't like to see things goin' to waste, do you, Your Honour?

MAGISTRATE: No.

BIDDY: No more do I, Your Honour. And so, I'd pick up the ones that'd fall on the ground and put 'em into a barrel. Then, to keep 'em from dryin' up, I'd put some water in with them – (and a few other things) and let 'em bide there.

MAGISTRATE: Water and a few other things. You had a recipe?

BIDDY: Oh, indeed I did, Your Honour. A recipe that me dear grandmother Molly Shannahan brought out with her from County Galway – and told it to me before she died.

MAGISTRATE: Twas an old recipe?

BIDDY: Old! Why, Your Honour, 'tis said that the Shannahan men-folk used to use it to cure snake-bite, and sure, that must have been a long time ago – even before the blessed Saint drove the slithery things out of Galway.

MAGISTRATE: But – Mrs. Muldoon. What use did you have for this – Snake-bite remedy?

BIDDY: Me, Your Honour? None at all. Nor Paddy neither, not in the matter of snake-bites. But we used it for medicine.

MAGISTRATE: Oh?

BIDDY: Yes, Your Honour – which brings me to the subject of Paddy's heart-burn.

PADDY: Biddy – Biddy darlin' –

CONSTABLE: Order there! Order.

MAGISTRATE: Yes, Mrs. Muldoon – gettin' back to the subject of Paddy's heart-burn.

BIDDY: Oh my, Your Honour, he suffers terrible from it, and he always says that a pint-mug of this berry-juice gives him blessèd relief.

MAGISTRATE: And what effect did a pint-mug of this – medicine have on Mr. Muldoon – apart of course, from relievin' his heart-burn?

BIDDY: None at all, Your Honour. Except for his fiddle.

MAGISTRATE: Except for his fiddle. Yes. Continue, Mrs. Muldoon.

BIDDY: Well, Your Honour, there we'd be, the two of us in the long winter evenin's – and I'd say to him, Paddy, I'd say – take down your fiddle and play some of the music of Old County Galway. And he'd say "Biddy darlin', I would only I've got another touch of the heart-burn." And so, Your Honour, I'd go and draw him off a pint mug-full (and sometimes two) until he got blessèd relief, and then he'd take his fiddle and play to bring the tears into me eyes – and his own too.

And what I can't understand, Your Honour, is why the Authorities should be down on poor Paddy about it.

MAGISTRATE: Did you ever give any of this to anybody besides Mr. Muldoon?

BIDDY: No. Your Honour. Never. Except once or twice – and then only to relieve pain.

PADDY: Biddy, darlin' –

CONSTABLE: Order, Order there.

MAGISTRATE: Tell me about – this "once or twice."

BIDDY: Well, Your Honour, 'twas one night when there was a weddin' on down in Hartley's Harbour and Obadiah Grimes and a few others came to me door and asked me if I had a drop of anything to give them for the weddin'. I told them "No" – that I wouldn't have the like in the house – that apart from water, I had nothin' but this drop of old berry juice.

MAGISTRATE: Did they want any of that?

BIDDY: At first they did, Your Honour, but when I explained that 'twas only good as a medicine for heart-burn they went away again. But, about an hour later Obadiah Grimes come back.

MAGISTRATE: Oh. He did?

BIDDY: Yes, Your Honour. He was all doubled up in pain.

MAGISTRATE: And what was wrong with him?

BIDDY: Heart-burn, Your Honour. And *was* he *sufferin'*! It took three or four mugfuls before he was properly eased. Then, when he was afraid he might get another attack in the middle of the night, I give him a quart-bottleful to take home with him.

MAGISTRATE: And he got away – all right?

BIDDY: Oh yes, Your Honour. I can prove he did.

MAGISTRATE: How?

BIDDY: Because I heard afterwards how he made a show of himself that night at the weddin', and how his wife Jemima was all upset over it.

MAGISTRATE: You don't think his behaviour had any connection with the – berry juice?

BIDDY: Of course not, Your Honour. It never affected Paddy that way. And now Your Honour –

MAGISTRATE: Yes.

BIDDY: About this recipe.

MAGISTRATE: Ah yes – the recipe.

BIDDY: It's likely to die with me, seein' as how I've got no women folks to hand it on to before I die.

MAGISTRATE: Oh, I imagine it's still preserved among the other Shannahans back in County Galway.

BIDDY: Did I do wrong in not givin' the recipe to the Constable when he asked me for it?

MAGISTRATE: Constable!

CONSTABLE: Yes – Your Honour.

MAGISTRATE: Did you –

CONSTABLE: Well – Your Honour – evidence – You see, Your Honour.

MAGISTRATE: Yes. I think I see. No, Mrs. Muldoon, you didn't do wrong. You don't have to give the recipe to anybody.

BIDDY: But I'll give it to Your Honour gladly.

MAGISTRATE: Will you indeed, Mrs. Muldoon? – I mean "No, thank you" Mrs. Muldoon. Even a magistrate needs to pray not to be led into temptation.

And now, stand aside while I deliver judgement on Patrick Muldoon.

BIDDY: Don't be hard on him, Your Honour – He's all I got.

MAGISTRATE: I'll take your plea into consideration, Mrs. Muldoon.

And now Patrick. The Court finds you guilty of the illegal possession of what the law in its wisdom calls Alcoholic Liquor, and the penalty in such case made and provided is that you serve a term of not less than seven days in jail, or pay a fine of not less than Ten Dollars. (Gasp from Biddy.)

Now there are a number of things I can do. I can sentence you to seven days, and with the jail almost a hundred miles up the shore, there's a reasonable chance of gettin' you there before your term expired. Or I could sentence you to a longer term and thereby penalize you for not anticipatin' the law and movin' your residence nearer to the jail-house. I am not impressed by either the wisdom of the one course or the justice of the other. So, Patrick, let's consider the matter of the ten dollar fine.

PADDY: Of course, Your Honour. Cash is out of the question.

MAGISTRATE: I understand.

PADDY: A few bags of cobblers later in the fall, Your Honour, or a few twenty-two pound tubs of black currants next summer.

MAGISTRATE: What have you got that the Court can take to sell and raise the money?

PADDY: Well, I want to help you out, Skipper Bob, Your Honour, but I'm blest if I can think of anything except me punt and me horse.

MAGISTRATE: You need your punt to make your living. What about your horse?

PADDY: Yes, you can take me horse and welcome.

MAGISTRATE: In good condition?

PADDY: The best, Your Honour. Not a wobble in either one of the four legs.

MAGISTRATE: Good for woods-work?

PADDY: That's all I ever used it for, Your Honour.

MAGISTRATE: Well then. That's how we'll settle it. Constable you're to take Mr. Muldoon's horse, sell it to some one of the woods contractors, retain ten dollars and give Mr. Muldoon what's left over.

CONSTABLE: But Your Honour.

MAGISTRATE: Yes, Constable.

CONSTABLE: He hasn't got a horse.

PADDY: I have so, Your Honour. The Constable saw it in me back-yard. It's been lyin' there these fifty years.

CONSTABLE: Your wood-horse?

PADDY: Yes. What other horse did you think I was talkin' about.

MAGISTRATE: Order – while I conclude my judgement.

Far be it from me to question the wisdom of those who make our laws and set minimum fines and jail terms, and further be it from me to anticipate the outcome of any subsequent action the Supreme Court might take on the verdict I'm about to pronounce. But this I must say, to wit.

The Court derives no pleasure from the prospect of the Muldoon household being afflicted with heart-burn and thereby being deprived of hearing the music of old County Galway. I might inject here, that since the Killicks came from County Antrim, I won't be accused by the Supreme Court of showing favouritism. So let's put it this way. Mrs. Muldoon, if you must have heart-burn medicine in your home, see to it that it's administered to in-patients only. On no account are you to conduct an out-patient department. And, Mrs. Muldoon!

BIDDY: Yes, Your Honour.

MAGISTRATE: Whatever you do, don't operate a travelling clinic.

Sentence is suspended.

Applause.

CONSTABLE: Order there! Order in the Court!

Break.

BEN: And Michael, that's the way it ended.

MICHAEL: I'd like to have met Skipper Bob.

BEN: You won't now. Not in this world. But Michael, we found out afterwards who it was that informed on the Muldoons.

MICHAEL: How?

BEN: Twas the following winter that Uncle Paddy was laid up with a twisted ankle, and Aunt Biddy had the flu' at the same time.

MICHAEL: What happened then?

BEN: Everybody wanted to help, but 'twas Jemima Grimes that took charge. She made Obe keep the Muldoons in firewood all that winter, and she herself come up here and kept house till Aunt Biddy was well. Aunt Biddy tried to thank her, but Jemima said she owed the Muldoons more than she'd ever live to pay.

MICHAEL: What happened to the recipe?

BEN: Well Michael, my guess is that it's still the secret of the Shannahan women folk back in County Galway.

What time is it, Michael? You're gettin' cold.

MICHAEL: Past five, Ben. Time to be getting back.

BEN: Yes. I s'pose so. Tide's up now. Ah. I was afraid of that.

MICHAEL: What?

BEN: Wind's in from the east'ard.

MICHAEL: Yes. It's turned chilly.

BEN: And we'll fly a drop of water gettin' back home. Nothin' to hurt, but a wettin' wouldn't do you any good. I think we'd better run before it to Hartley's Harbour. You can join the steamer there instead of Pigeon Inlet.

MICHAEL: But what about you?

BEN: I'll phone up and tell Lizzie I'm in Hartley's Harbour all right.

MICHAEL: What about your meeting tonight?

BEN: Oh, they can do without me one night.

MICHAEL: No, Ben. Don't miss it. Let's go home.

BEN: All right, but put on this oil-coat, sit up forrard and let me wrap this bear-skin round your knees.

MICHAEL: But I can't take your oil-coat.

BEN: Nonsense, Mike! I took a fellow's mackinaw one night. On a ice-pan.

MICHAEL: And this time – you take the tiller – shipmate.

BEN: Ay, ay – shipmate.

Break.

BEN: (It wasn't too bad goin' home. Just a dirty wind lop and a drop of spr'y back in the stern. But the main thing was I kept Michael dry and got him home with plenty of time to spare before the steamer was due or the Lodge meetin' either. After he went in, Soph come out to tell me what she'd been wantin' to tell me early that mornin'. And a fine time she picked to tell me that he was a clergyman. Yes. She'd noticed his collar that morning at breakfast time before he dressed up with the scarf around his neck. Of all things – a clergyman!

Well! That flustered me. What in the world did he think of me. Here I'd been all day callin' him by name just like he was a ordinary man. And the things I'd said. All right for one fisherman to say 'em to another. But to a clergyman. My oh my.

Well, if that flustered me, how do you think I felt when I got home – and found Lizzie – my own wife – lookin' and actin' as if she was cracked.)

Break.

LIZ: Ben. Ben. Oh, Ben.

BEN: Lizzie, Lizzie my dear. What's the matter?

LIZ: Ben. Oh how can I tell you –

BEN: Yes.

LIZ: I've seen a – vision.

BEN: A what?

LIZ: A vision. I tell you I've seen a vision. I've seen Maggie O'Rourke. She that I grew up with. That married Ferg Shannahan the day I married you – and that, oh Ben – that's been dead these forty-five years. I've seen her today.

BEN: Seen her? Where?

LIZ: Comin' up the path with you a few minutes ago.

BEN: Nonsense, Lizzie. That wasn't Maggie O'Rourke, nor any other Maggie. Calm down now. That was a man. A real man too.

LIZ: But Ben – what's his name?

BEN: His name is Michael. But I've just found out –

LIZ: Michael. Ben, please, run back to Sophy's and ask him, for my sake – if his name isn't Michael Shannahan.

BEN: Michael Shannahan! Well if I'm not the stupidest –

LIZ: Hurry Ben. Ask him isn't his name Michael Shannahan.

BEN: I'll do better than that Lizzie. I'll ask him isn't his name Michael Fergus Shannahan.

Break.

BEN: (He was sittin' by the fire in Sophy's dinin' room while she was gettin' his bit of supper ready in the kitchen. His top coat and scarf were off now and 'twas easy to see what he was. At first I couldn't get a word out, but he smiled at me and 'twas he that spoke first.)

MICHAEL: Hello – shipmate.

BEN: Sir – I'm ashamed.

MICHAEL: There's nothing to be ashamed of, Ben.

BEN: But sir – us people always show proper respect for the clergy – all clergy. And I didn't know.

MICHAEL: Now that it's over, I'm glad in a way that you didn't know. Perhaps, not seeing the collar, you had a better chance to see the man inside it.

BEN: I've a question to ask you, sir – if I might make so bold. Grandma, that's my missus wants me to ask you, sir, is your name Michael Shannahan?

MICHAEL: Yes. That's right.

BEN: Michael Fergus Shannahan?

MICHAEL: Yes.

BEN: The son of Ferg Shannahan and Maggie O'Rourke – that was.

MICHAEL: Yes. Do you know, Ben, there were many times today when I thought you had guessed it.

BEN: Ah, I was stun, sir. There were a dozen times today when you as good as told me. But Lizzie was smarter. She spotted you the minute she laid eyes on you comin' up the path. I've seen a vision she said. The vision of Maggie O'Rourke – Ask him, she said. Ask him if his name isn't Michael Shannahan.

She wants to see you, sir – that is, if you can spare a minute to a poor old woman before you go.

MICHAEL: Lizzie. That would be Lizzie Marshall – that was.

BEN: Yes, sir. Marshall it was before I married her. Now, sir, shall I tell her that your reverence will be comin' over to see her?

MICHAEL: No, Ben.

BEN: Oh.

MICHAEL: Tell her that Maggie O'Rourke's boy, Michael, will be coming over to see her.

Break.

BEN: (And come he did – the minute he could get away from Sophy's table. And through the kitchen-window, Grandma's eyes followed him every step of the way, from Soph's door to ours. I was uneasy that the excitement might be bad for her, but I needn't have worried. They met as if they'd been doin' it every day for years.)

MICHAEL: Hello, Aunt Lizzie.

LIZ: Hello, Michael.

MICHAEL: And how are you today, Aunt Lizzie?

LIZ: Poorly, Michael, poorly. Nothin' serious. It's just that the summers are not what they used to be.

MICHAEL: Indeed they're not, Aunt Lizzie.

LIZ: No. Here it is – three more days to the middle of July and the evenin's still airsome. But 'twill get warmer soon, and I'll be able to get out and help around the garden.

MICHAEL: I'm sure you will.

LIZ: Yes. And thank God I can still hobble around the house and get Ben's meals. Poor Ben. I'm afraid I'm not the help to him that I ought to be.

BEN: Now, Grandma, hush that kind of talk.

LIZ: But never mind my troubles, Michael. Tell me about yourself. You weren't even born when dear Maggie and Fergus went away. But – Maggie was expectin'. She told me. We used to tell each other everything.

MICHAEL: You were good friends, weren't you?

LIZ: Ah yes. We grew up together down in Marshall's Harbour. Always together in our wakin' hours. Except of course on Sundays when she'd go to Mass and I'd go to prayers. And whoever was out first'd wait for the other one. Ah – these were the times.

MICHAEL: Then – ?

LIZ: Then come the summer when Ferg and Ben come down fishin' out of Marshall's Harbour – and two summers later we come back here with 'em – married. My Sophy was born the followin' July, and dear Maggie was expectin' when she went away in August. She was hopin' for a boy – she was goin' to call him Michael.

MICHAEL: And she did.

LIZ: Ah, Michael – what a stock you sprung from. With the smile and the eyes of Maggie O'Rourke and the frame of Fergus Shannahan – what a man you are. And, Michael.

MICHAEL: Yes, Aunt Lizzie?

LIZ: I see you picked a good callin', my son – a good callin'. Did Maggie know before she died that you were goin' to do it?

MICHAEL: Yes.

LIZ: She must've been very happy. And Fergus? Is he –

MICHAEL: Twenty years ago.

LIZ: And Michael. Did Maggie ever tell you about me?

MICHAEL: Many's the time. And today I'm keeping a promise I made her.

LIZ: There's something of Maggie's right here in this house. Something you've never seen, and that I want to show you. But first of all Michael, tell me – can't you bide a bit longer?

MICHAEL: I wish I could, Aunt Lizzie.

LIZ: But, won't you be comin' back to us again?

MICHAEL: I'd like to, but – no.

LIZ: Oh. Oh well, I'll always thank the Blessèd Lord for sendin' you this time. Now. Here's what I want to show you. Come over here by the window, where the light is best.

MICHAEL: Yes.

LIZ: Look – Here on the window-sill. In the flower-pot.

MICHAEL: What a lovely flower. A begonia, isn't it?

LIZ: A begonia it is. And well nigh as lovely as her that owned it sixty years ago.

MICHAEL: Maggie?

LIZ: Bless your heart – yes! The day before she and Ferg left, she came up to see me, where I was confined with Sophy bein' only ten days old. "Lizzie darlin'" she said "take this flower and keep it alive as long as you can as a reminder of me." And I've kept it alive – sixty years. It'll live as long as I will.

MICHAEL: I didn't think a flower could live so long.

LIZ: Ah yes, if it's cared for, Michael, I've watered it every day, changed the earth on it every spring, and taken a new slip off it before ever the old stem could die. Michael.

MICHAEL: Yes, Aunt Lizzie.

LIZ: Let's you and me water it.

MICHAEL: I'd love to.

LIZ: Well then, we'll do it. Ben'll fetch a jugful of water – the little lustre jug, Ben. Thank you, dear. Now, Michael, you pour some water on it and I'll pour some. No – not there on the top – pour it into the dish at the bottom.

MICHAEL: Oh, you water it from the bottom.

LIZ: Always. And the lamp wick carries the water from the dish – up through the hole in the bottom of the pot. Just keep the dish moistened, and the wick'll do the rest.

MICHAEL: There. Is that enough?

LIZ: That's your part. Now I'll pour a drop or two for good measure. Ben, dear, hand over the scissors. Now, Michael, there's one other thing. Take the scissors. Open them. That's right. Now, hold them just below the joint on that little branch. Not too close. There, that's it. Now. Snip!

MICHAEL: There you are. I've done it. What next?

LIZ: Stand the little branch in the jug with the water we didn't use. That's it. Thank you, Michael. In a few days, I'll plant that slip and there'll be two pots and two begonias in the window. You see, dear, there's no longer just Maggie – There's Maggie and Michael. (*Distant sound of a steamer's whistle, followed by guns firing, nearby.*) We did it just in time. And you must go?

MICHAEL: Yes.

LIZ: God bless you, Michael.

MICHAEL: And you, Aunt Lizzie. Remember me in your prayers.

LIZ: Indeed I will.

MICHAEL: Now I must say good-bye to Sophy. She was very kind.

BEN: And I'll go and get your suitcase –

– Oh, here's Skipper Joe. What are the guns firin' about, Joe? Is the Federal member aboard the steamer or have the turrs come in?

JOE: Neither – that we know for. But 'tis got around that Ferg Shannahan's son is here and we'm givin' him a Newfoundland send-off. We didn't have long enough notice to build a arch. Be you Ferg's son, sir?

MICHAEL: Yes, Joe.

JOE: Well, well, well. And you can't stay? We'd like to have got to know 'ee better sir. We're awful sorry.

MICHAEL: I'm sorry too Joe. Tell them "God Bless them all."

Break.

BEN: (And a few minutes later, he was sittin' in the stern of the mail boat, smilin' and wavin' good-bye to the crowd on the wharf. We watched him board the steamer and watched the steamer till she went around the Point.

That night on the way home from the Lodge, Skipper Joe said to me.)

JOE: Grampa. Mark my words. We've seen him for the first and last times.

BEN: Oh. I don't know.

JOE: Grampa. I was figgerin'. I'm a year older than him, and have been through plenty of hardship – and hard times.

BEN: Yes, Joe?

JOE: But the minute I laid eyes on that man, I could see that he's been through more hardship than I've ever been through. And – it's shortened his days.

BEN: But he didn't mention any hardships.

JOE: No. He wouldn't.

Break.

BEN: (Well, after that, things in Pigeon Inlet went on much as usual. Lizzie had two begonia plants to tend instead of one. Then one day – a Tuesday it was – the first flower bloomed on Michael's plant. I was almost as excited as she was, although I wouldn't let on. I told her she was fussin' more than when Soph's daughter Soos was born.

Then about two weeks later – the letter come.)

BEN: Liz – here's a letter I just got from the Post Office.

LIZ: My. Our cheques have come early this month.

BEN: 'Tis not that kind of a envelope.

LIZ: Who's it for? You or me?

BEN: Looks like it's addressed to both of us. Here. I'll open it. You read it. Here's your glasses. Well – read it. Ain't you goin' to read it? Here my dear. I'll pick it up. Now – Read it out. Is it from – Michael?

LIZ: No.

BEN: Is it about Michael?

LIZ: Yes.

BEN: Oh.

LIZ: The flower is beautiful, isn't it Ben?

BEN: Lovely, my dear.

LIZ: I'll read the letter.

    Dear Mr. and Mrs. Walcott: This is to inform you regretfully that his Excellency, Bishop Michael Fergus Shannahan passed away three days ago. His passing was not unexpected. He had never recovered from his harrowing experiences in the Far Eastern prison camp, and he was happy to have fulfilled a long cherished hope by visiting you before the end came. He left two personal messages for me to send to you. They were: "To Aunt Lizzy – I believe our begonia has blossomed." "To Uncle Ben – " Here Ben I can't read this part.

BEN: Doesn't matter dear. I know what it is. *"Caelum non animum mutant, qui trans mare currunt."*

LIZ: Why, Ben. I believe that is what it reads like. But how –

BEN: That's our password dear. Michael's and mine. Just like the begonia – his and yours. So he's gone.

LIZ: Yes, Ben.

BEN: A far eastern prison. The cusséd heathens. They shortened his days.

LIZ: Hush, Ben. Don't say that. The poor unfortunate heathens. They didn't know Michael like we did, or they'd never have done it.

BEN: But what was it the letter called Michael?

LIZ: His Excellency Bishop Michael Fergus Shannahan.

BEN: A Bishop. And I didn't know.

LIZ: I knew – by the purple under his collar.

BEN: You should've told me. So's I could have respected him more.

LIZ: You couldn't have, Ben. Nor loved him more neither.

BEN: That's right.

LIZ: Oh, Ben.

BEN: Yes?

LIZ: He passed away Tuesday – week afore last.

BEN: Yes?

LIZ: The begonia – his and mine!

BEN: What about it?

LIZ: Oh, Ben. It flowered – that very day.

BEN: (And now a year has gone, and like I said, I'm sittin' on my stage-head lookin' at Skipper Joe Irwin's schooner – and thinkin'. Thinkin' about how weak are the things that try to pull men apart – differences in colours, creeds, and opinions – weak things like the ripples tuggin' at the schooner's chain. And thinkin' about how strong are the things that hold men together – strong, like Joe's anchor, and chain, and the good holdin' ground below. Why, in Pigeon Inlet we've got things stronger even than dyin'. The things that brought Michael back from a heathen prison to eat mussels on Muldoon's Cove beach – the things that are takin' me tomorrow to put a lick of paint on the fence round the graves of the Cassidys, the Muldoons – and the Shannahans.

But, I'm gettin' too old to be goin' away alone. I need someone with me – for company – and to do it after I'm gone.) Oh. Good evenin' Skipper Joe.

JOE: Evenin' Grampa.

BEN: I was just watchin' your schooner, Joe – swingin' about this way – Never keeps still. Looks almost like she's adrift.

JOE: Nah! Good holdin'-ground there. Besides, 'tis not in a schooner's nature to keep still. Except when she's high and dry – rottin' on the beach.

BEN: Busy tomorrow, Joe?

JOE: Oh, not very. We've got one trap up and the crew can handle what we're likely to get in the other. Why?

BEN: I was wonderin' if you'd come to Muldoon's Cove with me.

JOE: Tomorrow?

BEN: Yes. 'Twill be just a year tomorrow since I was there

46

with Michael, and I thought I should go down again to look at the cemetery fence. You know – a lick of paint and a palin' here and there to be nailed on.

JOE: Sure I'll come. I'll be glad to.

BEN: Now, Joe. Come into my stage. I've got something to show you. There. I'm thinkin' about tackin' that piece of board to the cemetery fence.

JOE: Fine piece of pine board – You've painted it black – with white letterin' on it. It says – hey, I can't read this stuff. What is it?

BEN: I think it's Latin, Joe.

JOE: Oh. That's a horse of a different colour.

BEN: Why, Joe?

JOE: I don't know as I approve of this Latin stuff. Where did you get it from?

BEN: Bishop Michael told me last year. Then afterwards 'twas on a letter sent to us after he died. I copied out the letters and painted them on the board. I thought 'twould be nice to nail it up on their cemetery fence.

JOE: Still. I'm not sure I agree with Latin. Know what it means?

BEN: Yes. Michael told me. It says *"Caelum non animum mutant, qui trans mare currunt."*

JOE: Yes but what do it mean?

BEN: It means "You can take a man out of the Bay, but you can't take the Bay out of the man."

JOE: Oh – (pause) Ben?

BEN: Yes, Joe.

JOE: Was you thinkin' about nailin' that board to the fence?

BEN: Yes. Why?

JOE: Pity to use nails on that good pine. I'll bring along some brass screws. Just the right length. Keep it up longer too. What time do we go tomorrow?

BEN: Early, Joe. Don't forget Lodge tomorrow night.

JOE: I'll run up the flag before we leave. Well, I must be gettin' home. Awful chilly for this time of year.

BEN: Yes, another three or four days and 'twill be the middle of July.

JOE: Yes. Summers are not like they used to be. So long, Grampa.

BEN: So long – Joe.